BRADLEY WIGGINS

Roy Apps

Illustrated by Chris Kin...

D0993868

LONDON·SYDNEY

First published in 2012 by
Franklin Watts
338 Euston Road
London NW1 3BH

Franklin Watts Australia
Level 17/207 Kent Street
Sydney NSW 2000

Text © Roy Apps 2012
Illustrations © Chris King 2012
Cover design by Peter Scoulding

The author and illustrator have asserted their rights in accordance
with the Copyright, Designs and Patents Act, 1988.

All rights reserved.

A CIP catalogue record for this book
is available from the British Library.

ISBN: 978 1 4451 1831 4

1 3 5 7 9 10 8 6 4 2

Printed in Great Britain

Franklin Watts is a division of Hachette Children's Books,
an Hachette UK company.
www.hachette.co.uk

ROTHERHAM LIBRARY SERVICE	
B53031476	
Bertrams	15/10/2012
JN	£5.99
SLS	J920 WIG

Chapter One:

Hooked!

The striker had a clear sight of the goal: chalk lines on a wall of the block of flats. He was about to shoot, when suddenly a hand grabbed his shirt and he was hustled to the ground.

"Penalty!"

It was just a kickabout really. There was no referee. Eventually, it was agreed that it was a penalty — but nobody expected it to be scored. The goalkeeper was something special, the best around. He was tall, athletic and seemed to have springs for feet. He'd spent the summer holidays at the West Ham United Soccer School, and everyone reckoned he would go on to be a top professional.

There was a moment's silence as everyone got ready for the penalty kick to be taken. The goalkeeper stood firm between the chalk mark goalposts. Then:

"Bradley!" yelled a woman from the balcony above. "Time you came in."

"Oh, Mum!" groaned the goalkeeper. "Can't I stay out a bit longer?"

"In!" said the goalkeeper's mum, firmly. "Now!"

The goalkeeper trudged off. He was aware of his mates chuckling and sniggering behind him.

When he got back to the flat, he saw that the TV was on.

"There's something I want you to watch," said his mum.

It was the Olympics, live from Barcelona.

"And at last, the moment everyone in Britain has been waiting for," the commentator was saying. "The men's individual track pursuit final!"

"This is it, Bradley," whispered his mum excitedly. "It's the top event in track cycling."

Bradley and his mum watched as the two riders sped round the cycle track. One bike stood out — it looked like something from a sci-fi movie. The rider's helmet was weird, too. It had a

long point at the back going all the way down his neck. But the cyclist on the sci-fi bike soon powered past reigning world champion, Jens Lehmann.

"And it's gold for Chris Boardman, and for Great Britain!" screamed the commentator.

While his mum leapt around the room, whooping with delight, Bradley sat there staring at the TV. He couldn't take his eyes off Chris Boardman and his amazing Lotus super machine.

Bradley Wiggins was twelve years old, and he was hooked on bikes.

Chapter Two:
The Helmet

A few weeks later, Bradley propped up his bike in the hall. It didn't look much like Chris Boardman's amazing machine, but it was all he had. He didn't even have a helmet, and he knew his mum hadn't got the money to buy one. She had brought him up alone, ever since his dad had left home.

He went into the kitchen and sat down.

"Are you all right, Bradley?"

Bradley looked at his mum. "Tell me about my dad," he said, quietly.

"Do you remember him at all?"

Bradley shook his head.

"One day when you were just two years old," his mum began, "your dad upped and left us. I had no money and no home, so you and I went to live with your gran and grandad. Then I managed to get a job and this flat. But you want to know about your dad's cycling, don't you?"

Bradley nodded.

"Your dad was a professional cyclist. He did track cycling. That draws big crowds in Europe. But road racing was your dad's real love. He used to say that when you're doing a road event, you live the race. But it was a hard life. Sometimes, to make ends meet, he would do a night shift in a warehouse and then compete in a 200 km road race during the day. This might be for three or four days a week. Your dad was tough and he worked hard."

Later that day, Bradley went round to see his grandad. He told him he wanted to become a racing cyclist. He told him he hadn't got a helmet.

Bradley's grandad thought for a moment, then he said: "Come with me. I think I might be able to help you out."

They went into the shed at the bottom of the small garden. Bradley's grandad hunted about, muttering to himself. Then, suddenly, he yelled: "Yes! I knew I'd still got it somewhere."

He was waving around a very old and very battered cycling helmet.

"This belonged to your dad," Bradley's grandad said.

Bradley tried it on.

It fitted. Perfectly.

Chapter Three:
Crash!

The following month, Bradley's mum took him along to the Archer Road Cycling Club in South London.

"I'm really pleased that you're keen

on cycling," she said. "But the track is the best place for a boy of your age to do it. London's roads are far too dangerous."

At Archer Road, the man in charge looked Bradley up and down. He glanced at the boy's bike and sighed.

"Well, I suppose we can do something with you. What's your name?"

"Bradley."

"Surname?"

"Wiggins."

The man put his pen down and looked at Bradley. "Wiggins? You're not related to Garry Wiggins, by any chance?"

"He's my dad," said Bradley.

"People in the world of cycling still talk about him," said the man. "How's he doing these days?"

"I don't know," said Bradley. "I've not seen him since I was two."

Soon, Bradley was spending every spare moment he had cycling. One cold and dark winter's evening, he told his mum he was going to ride across to Ealing in West London for a cycle meet.

"Not on your bike, you're not," said his mum. "It's a dreadful night out there. And it's rush hour. You can go on the bus."

"Real cyclists don't go by bus!" protested Bradley.

"But you're only twelve!" his mum replied.

He and his mum had a row. Bradley stormed out of the flat and dragged his bike down the stairs.

He was halfway to Ealing when he pulled out to go round a bus that had stopped to pick up some passengers. At the same time, a car pulled out to turn right. It smashed straight into Bradley. He went right over the top of the car and hit the ground with a sickening thud.

People rushed over to help. They found him in a twisted heap — he wasn't moving.

Chapter Four:

Racer

Bradley opened his eyes. Through the bright lights above his head he saw his mum. She was crying.

"Oh, Bradley!" she whispered.

"Have I missed the cycle meet?" Bradley asked. He was aware that his voice sounded croaky and quiet.

"Cycle meet!" Bradley's mum's voice was louder now. "You're in no fit shape to go to a cycle meet. You're in hospital with a broken collarbone and concussion."

As soon as Bradley was out of hospital he went to see his grandad.

"You were in a bad way, son," said his grandad. "But I'm afraid your bike came off even worse."

Bradley looked at the twisted pile of metal in his grandad's shed. It was hardly recognisable as a bike. Bradley knew that there was no money in his family for a new bike. How could he become a racing cyclist without a bike? It seemed he would have to give up his dream. He fought back the tears.

Back home, his mum said: "Come on, Bradley, we're going shopping."

Bradley sighed. His day had started badly, and was slowly getting worse.

Bradley hated shopping. It was so boring.

"Well, Bradley, what do you think?" his mum called.

Bradley saw that she was looking into a large shop window that was crammed full of bikes.

"It's about time you had a proper racing bike," said his mum, a huge grin spreading across her face.

Bradley looked at the price tags on the bikes in the window. "B—But we can't afford one of those!"

"We can now," replied his mum. "I got a cheque in the post this morning. Compensation money from the driver of the car which knocked you down."

There was no stopping Bradley Wiggins now. He raced at different tracks in London most nights of the week, and if the weather was fine, at weekends, too. With his new racing bike he quickly became established as a top teenage rider.

When he was seventeen, he won the Junior Track Cycling World Championships 2 km individual pursuit event. Three years later, aged just twenty, he won a bronze medal in the team track pursuit event at the Sydney 2000 Olympic Games.

Chapter Five:
Rock Bottom

In 2002, Bradley signed up as a professional rider with top team, *FD Jeux*, based in France. They attracted the best riders from all over the world.

But Bradley was young, and a junior member of the team. It was the senior riders who got to compete in all the big races. The team's top rider was one of the best in the world, an Australian called Brad McGee. He'd even won a stage of the most famous road race of all, the Tour de France.

Bradley was left to train on his own. At race meetings, he stood unnoticed at the side of the track watching Brad McGee as he was applauded and cheered after each race he won. Gradually, Bradley started to believe that he was useless. He thought he'd never become a top rider like Brad McGee.

Bradley returned home to train with Team GB for the 2002 Commonwealth Games in Manchester. He started to feel a bit better about himself. He had an Olympic bronze medal, after all.

But when the details of the Commonwealth Games Individual Pursuit were announced, any newfound confidence Bradley thought he had quickly disappeared. He was down to race against Brad McGee!

There was an enormous home crowd

at the Manchester Velodrome to cheer
Bradley on. But it made no difference.
Bradley didn't see or hear them. All
he could see was the man he was
competing against, the star rider for his
team back in France, Brad McGee.

Bradley could have given him a race;
could have tried to get a personal best
time for himself. He didn't. He lost,
badly, and to the crowd in Manchester
and the millions watching on TV, it
looked as if he wasn't really trying.
He was called in for a meeting with
the Team GB management.

"What's wrong with you, Bradley?"

How could he tell them he was spooked by the great Brad McGee? He just shrugged.

"Look, if you ride as badly as you've been doing, there's no way you'll make the cut for the Athens Olympics in 2004. Maybe we should try to get you a mentor."

"Do what you like," muttered Bradley.

He'd not been home long when the phone rang.

"Bradley?"

"Yeah."

"It's Chris Boardman."

Bradley thought he was hearing things.

Chris Boardman? The most famous British rider of all time? The man who had inspired him to race, when he'd been just a kid? What was he doing on the phone?

"Team GB have asked me to become your mentor," Chris Boardman explained. "I think we need to talk."

Chapter Six:
Back on the Road

It took a long time, but working with Chris Boardman finally paid off for Bradley. At the 2004 Olympics in Athens he won gold, silver and bronze medals; the first British athlete in 40 years to win three medals at one Games. At the 2008 Olympics in Beijing he won two golds for track events.

That year, Bradley heard that his dad had died in Australia. He'd seen his dad a few times, but their meetings had never been a success. Bradley's stepsister had told him that his dad had been really proud of him. Bradley was just sad that his dad hadn't been able to tell him that himself.

One day, when Bradley was in London visiting his mum, he said to her: "Do you remember that time when I was a kid and we watched Chris Boardman winning his gold medal on the telly?"

His mum smiled.

"You told me about dad's racing. How his real love had been road racing, because there you lived the race?"

His mum nodded.

"I think I know what he meant," Bradley said, quietly.

Bradley had done a fair bit of road racing himself. He loved being amongst a large pack of riders, of being in his own little world for hours on end, then suddenly coming across a crowd of cheering spectators lining the road.

"If your dream is to become a top road racer," said his mum, "there's only one race you need to be thinking about: the Tour de France."

Bradley concentrated on his road racing. In the 2009 Tour de France, he finished fourth. The following year he could only finish twenty-fourth. Maybe the Tour de France wasn't for him.

But in 2011 Bradley won the British National Road Race Championships. It was his final race before that year's Tour de France. He had hit top form at just the right time.

He started the Tour de France superbly, and at the end of stage six he was lying sixth overall. Then disaster struck. He was in the middle of a large group, when a rider at the front fell. Some other riders crashed into him, Bradley amongst them.

He was left lying motionless and badly injured in the middle of the road.

Chapter Seven:
Triumph!

Bradley had broken his collarbone in the crash. But just two months later, he came third in the 3,300 km-long Vuelta a España. Bradley continued to train hard while his collarbone healed. In the dark winter evenings, after saying good night to his wife and two children, he walked out of the back door and down the garden to his shed.

Inside the shed was a racing bike on rollers. Bradley climbed on the bike and started pedalling, hard. Bradley was in serious training. It was lonely work, but he had a dream. To do better than fourth place in the 2012 Tour de France.

Nobody in the small Lancashire town of Eccleston, apart from his family, his friends and his coach, knew that Bradley was there. The rest of the world had forgotten him.

But, a few months later, that all changed. In the 2012 Tour de France, he took the yellow jersey by finishing third on stage 7. By the time he won the stage 19 time trial, everybody had heard of Bradley Wiggins. As he cycled triumphantly into Paris, he became the first British rider to win the Tour de France.

He barely had time to celebrate. Ten days later he found himself in southwest London, just a short distance from where he had lived as a boy. He was there to take part in the London 2012 Olympic Games Road Time Trial.

As Bradley set off on the 44 km ride, he knew that Tony Martin, the rider

who had beaten him at the Road World Championships the previous year, had set a very good time. At the 9 km mark, Martin was ahead. But Bradley was beginning to sense a special kind of atmosphere at this event. The crowds along the route were all cheering and waving Union flags. Bradley bent his head down over the handlebars. By 18 km he was 11 seconds ahead.

At 29 km he was 23 seconds ahead.

Along the final stretch of the route at Hampton Court, the crowds were packed five people deep. Their cheers turned to roars and screams as Bradley crossed the finishing line an incredible 46 seconds faster than Tony Martin in second place. It was Bradley's fourth Olympic gold medal.

Bradley Wiggins had achieved his dream. He had become the most successful British cyclist of all time.

Fact file
Bradley Wiggins

Full name: Bradley Marc Wiggins

Born: 28 April 1980, Ghent, Belgium

Height: 1.90 metres

Nickname: "Wiggo"

First Major Win
— 1997 UCI Junior Track Cycling World Championships
Gold, 2km Individual Pursuit

Olympic Medals

— 2000 Sydney Olympics
Bronze, Team Pursuit

— 2004 Athens Olympics
Gold, 4km Individual Pursuit
Silver, Team Pursuit
Bronze, Madison

— 2008 Beijing Olympics
Gold, 4km Individual Pursuit
Gold, Team Pursuit

— 2012 London Olympics
Gold, Olympic Road Time Trial

Other Achievements

- Bradley was 1st overall in the 2012 Tour de France
- With seven medals, Bradley is Great Britain's joint most decorated Olympian, along with Sir Chris Hoy
- 93rd most successful Olympian of all-time
- Only cyclist to have won the Tour de France and an Olympic Gold medal in the same year
- First ever British Winner of the Tour de France – the greatest cycling race of all

Rebecca Adlington

The 14-year-old girl stood on the side of the pool in the final of the 2003 European Youth Olympics 800 metres freestyle. As the swimmers dived in, the arena echoed noisily with shouts and cheers from the spectators. "Come on, Becks!" shouted the girl's family from their seats in the crowd. The girl touched the finishing wall in second place. Afterwards, her family and friends crowded around to congratulate her for winning the silver medal. A man approached the girl's mum. "That was a brilliant race your daughter swam," he said. "I think she's got potential. My name's Bill Furniss, by the way. I'm a professional swimming coach and I'd like to offer to coach your daughter."

Continue reading this story in:
DREAM TO WIN:
Rebecca Adlington